# THE WAY OF LIBERATION

# THE WAY OF
# $\mathcal{L}$IBERATION

~

## A PRACTICAL GUIDE TO
## SPIRITUAL ENLIGHTENMENT

# ADYASHANTI

Open Gate Sangha
San Jose, California

Open Gate Sangha, Inc.
Post Office Box 112107
Campbell, California 95011
www.opengatesangha.org

Cover and book design by Susan Kurtz and Maja Apolonia Rodé

Printed in the United States of America

ISBN: 978-1-937195-17-5

10 9 8 7 6 5 4 3 2 1

♻ This book is printed on recycled paper with 30% post-consumer waste.

# TABLE OF CONTENTS

# PREFACE

This book is a clue left behind, a means of remembrance, and a guide to waking up from your imagined status as a person to what you really are. The teachings contained within this book are a condensed version of my core teachings. In order for the teaching to have any effect, you must apply it with utmost dedication. Be forewarned, applying these teachings may be damaging to your beliefs, disorienting to your mind, and distressing to your ego. From the perspective of waking up to reality these are good things to be cultivated. From the perspective of ego they are to be avoided at all costs. The choice is entirely yours.

# INTRODUCTION

*T*he Way of Liberation is a stripped-down, practical guide to spiritual liberation, sometimes called awakening, enlightenment, self-realization, or simply seeing what is absolutely True. It is impossible to know what words like *liberation* or *enlightenment* mean until you realize them for yourself. This being so, it is of no use to speculate about what enlightenment is; in fact, doing so is a major hindrance to its unfolding. As a guiding principle, to progressively realize what is *not* absolutely True is of infinitely more value than speculating about what is.

Many people think that it is the function of a spiritual teaching to provide answers to life's biggest questions, but actually the opposite is true. The primary task of any good spiritual teaching is not to answer your questions, but to question your answers. For it is your conscious and unconscious assumptions and beliefs that distort your perception and cause you to see separation and division where there is actually only unity and completeness.

The Reality that these teachings are pointing toward is not hidden, or secret, or far away. You cannot earn it, deserve it, or figure it out. At this very moment, Reality and completeness are in plain sight. In fact, the only thing there is to see, hear, smell, taste, touch, or feel, is Reality, or God if you like. Absolute completeness surrounds you wherever you go. So there is really no reason to bother yourself about it, except for the fact that we humans have long ago deceived ourselves into such a confined tangle of confusion and disarray that we scarcely even consider, much less experience for ourselves, the divinity within and all around us.

The Way of Liberation is a call to action; it is something you *do. It is a doing that will undo you absolutely.* If you do not *do* the teaching, if you do not study and apply it fearlessly, it cannot effect any transformation. The Way of Liberation is not a belief system; it is something to be put into practice. In this sense it is entirely practical.

To read this book as a spectator would be to miss the point. Being a spectator is easy and safe; being an active participant in your own awakening to Truth is neither easy nor safe. The way forward is unpredictable, the commitment absolute, the results not guaranteed. Did you really think that it could be any other way?

If you compare The Way of Liberation to other teachings, or interpret it through the lens of other teachings, you will inevitably misinterpret The Way to be something that it is not. In the modern age, with its instant access to all the world's spiritual teachings, this is an especially pervasive problem. People often misinterpret what I say because they are filtering it through the lens of other spiritual teachings that may use a similar vocabulary. Therefore, I suggest that you approach these teachings on their own merit without filtering them through the mind's previous understanding.

No spiritual teaching is a direct path to enlightenment. In fact, there is no such thing as a path to enlightenment, simply because enlightenment is ever present in all places and at all times. What you *can do* is to remove any and all illusions, especially the ones you value most and find the most security in, that cloud your perception of Reality. Let go of clinging to your illusions and resisting what is, and Reality will suddenly come into view.

The Way of Liberation is medicine used to cure various states of spiritual dis-ease. Just as medicine is not itself good health but a means to good health, these teachings are not Truth but a means of revealing Truth. The Indian sage Ramana Maharshi likened spiritual teachings to thorns used to remove other thorns, and I rather like that image.

To study The Way of Liberation teachings is to study yourself. To study yourself does not mean to add more knowledge to your cluttered brain's ideas about yourself, but to remove all of the customary defining characteristics you usually associate self with: name, race, gender, occupation, social status, past, as well as all of the psychological judgments you make about yourself. When the self is stripped down to its essential core, all that can be said about it is: "I am; I exist."

What then is the I that exists?

This is not a book about spiritual betterment, self-improvement, or altered states of consciousness. It is about spiritual awakening, going from the dream state of ego to the awakened state beyond ego as quickly and efficiently as possible. The journey isn't what anyone anticipates, and enlightenment isn't what it is frequently sold as. I won't be telling you how to achieve bliss or unending happiness, find your soul mate, or the ten easy steps to making a quick million bucks. I don't believe in deceptive advertising or luring in spiritual seekers with false promises. Many spiritual seekers already live on a steady diet of spiritual junk food, those nice-sounding platitudes that have little or no transforming effect other than to dull the dissatisfaction inherent in the dream state. If you like that sort of thing, this isn't the book for you.

I have left clues to realizing Reality throughout this entire book, from the first page to the last. Do not assume that the most important elements of this teaching are easy to spot or clearly emphasized. They are woven into this book as threads are woven into fabric, easy to miss if you do not have the eyes to see or the sincerity to understand. This is not because I want to be obscure—I do everything I can to *not* be obscure—but because Truth is not something that can be truly and deeply understood by having it spoon-fed to you. Such truth is like fast food, easy to access but hardly satisfying in the long run.

In our modern society we expect to have everything given to us in easy-to-consume bite-size portions, preferably very quickly so that we can get on with our hurried lives. But Truth will not conform itself to our frantic avoidance of Reality or our desire to have the whole of something for the very least investment of time and energy.

You will get out of The Way of Liberation teachings exactly what you put into them. These teachings need to be studied, contemplated, and put into practice, not simply read as entertainment. As a wise person once said, "The proof of a desire is found in the habit of response."

It should also be understood that The Way of Liberation is neither a form of psychotherapy nor a cure-all for all the challenges that human beings face in their daily lives. While such therapeutic applications may be necessary and useful for some people, they are not the focus of this teaching.

Awakening is neither a magic cure for all that ails you, nor an escape from the difficulties of life. Such magical thinking runs contrary to the unfolding of Reality and is a great impediment to its mature expression. The aim of this teaching is to wake up to the absolute nature of Reality, then embody and live it to the fullest extent possible. Such awakening does eventually bring a sense of deep peace, love, and well-being, but these are the by-products of the awakened state, not the goal.

It is not the pursuit of greater and greater states of happiness and bliss that leads to enlightenment, but the yearning for Reality and the rabid dissatisfaction with living anything less than a fully authentic life.

## WAKE UP OR PERISH

The world's problems are, by and large, human problems—the unavoidable consequence of egoic sleepwalking. If we care to look, all the signs are present to suggest that we are not only sleepwalking, but at times borderline insane as well. In a manner of speaking, we have lost (or at the very least forgotten) our souls, and we try very, very hard not to notice, because we don't want to see how asleep we are, how desolate our condition really is. So we blindly carry on, driven by forces we do not recognize or understand, or even acknowledge.

We are no doubt at a very critical point in time. Our world hangs in the balance, and a precarious balance it is. Awakening to Reality is no longer a possibility; it is an imperative. We have sailed the ship of delusion about as far as she can carry us. We have run her ashore and now find ourselves shipwrecked on an increasingly desolate land. Our options have imploded. "Wake up or perish" is the spiritual call of our times. Did we ever need more motivation than this?

And yet all is eternally well, and more well than can be imagined.

# CHAPTER ONE

# THE FIVE FOUNDATIONS

*T*he Five Foundations are the bedrock on which the teaching rests. They should not be ignored, skimmed over, or taken lightly. In a very real sense the Five Foundations are *absolutely essential components* of the teaching that apply *after awakening* as much as, if not more than, before it. Don't be deceived into thinking that the Five Foundations are insignificant or rudimentary simply because they appear to be attuned more to the human, or relative, aspect of Reality. The Five Foundations are a means of *living* and *manifesting* the ultimate nature of Reality in daily life. If we do not live and manifest in our lives what we realize in our deepest moments of revelation, then we are living a split life.

Furthermore, the Five Foundations provide the context within which the teachings unfold. If you remove the context from the teaching, you are removing the anti-egoic safeguards that protect the teaching from egocentric interpretation. Misinterpretation of a spiritual teaching by the ego is always a significant danger, since the ego's tendency is to justify whatever points of view it is attached to and invested in.

To add to this danger, any spiritual teaching rooted in the absolute nature of Reality is by definition oriented toward Truth, not toward the ethical and moral dimension of relative life. This does not mean that such teachings are immoral, it means that they are trans-moral; that is, rooted in a Reality beyond the relative moral and ethical standards of the dualistic perspective.

This does not mean that all morality is rendered irrelevant in the absolute view; this is a common misunderstanding. It means that morality is no longer rooted in the cultural and religious values designed to rein in and control egoic impulses. Instead, selfless love and compassion naturally flow out of the unified view of Reality as spontaneous expressions of that unity. When nothing is seen to be separate or other than you, the actions that flow through you reflect that unified perspective.

It can get complicated because it is possible to have *some* experience of the ultimate nature of Reality while at the same time not being completely free of egoic delusion. This makes for the possible volatile mixture of Reality and illusion simultaneously existing and expressing itself in an unconscious and distorted way. While some of this is to be expected as we are maturing in spirit, there are few things more distorted or dangerous than an ego that thinks it is God.

Many years of working with thousands of people have shown me that if these foundational aspects of the spiritual life are ignored, it will almost always derail one's spiritual unfolding to some degree. A failure to explore and come to clarity about any one of these, as well as to consistently apply them, will result in ongoing inner and outer conflict and division at some level.

The Five Foundations are a means of gathering all of your inner resources—body, mind, and spirit—and focusing them in a unified way toward your highest aspiration. I cannot overemphasize the importance of having a clear unified focus, sincere heart, and an unwavering desire not to knowingly delude yourself or others.

## CLARIFY YOUR ASPIRATION

To clarify your aspiration means knowing exactly what it is that your spiritual life aspires to, *not as a future goal but in each moment.* In other words, what do you value most in your life—not in the sense of moral values, but in the sense of what is most important to you. Contemplate this question. Do not assume that you know what your highest aspiration is, or even what is most important to you. Dig deep within, contemplate, and meditate on what the spiritual quest is about for you; don't let anyone else define your aspiration for you. Look within until you find, with complete clarity, what you aspire to.

The importance of this first Foundation cannot be overemphasized, because life unfolds along the lines of what you value most. Very few people have Truth or Reality as deep values. They may think that they value Truth, but their actions do not bear this out. Generally, most people have competing and conflicting values, which manifest as both internal and external conflict. So just because you *think* something is your deepest value does not mean that it actually is. By deeply contemplating and clarifying what you value and aspire to, you become more unified, clear, and certain of your direction.

As your realization and spiritual maturity deepen, you will find that some aspects of your aspiration remain steadfast while others evolve to reflect what is relevant to your current level of insight. By reflecting on and clarifying the issues relevant to your *current* level of understanding, you stay focused on the cutting edge of your own unfolding.

## UNCONDITIONAL FOLLOW-THROUGH

Making clear what you aspire to is the first step. It has the effect of gathering energy and attention together into a unified force and directing it toward your aspiration. Once you have clarified your aspiration, you now need to follow through on it. Following through has to do with what you are *willing to do* or *let go of doing.*

Spirituality does not require that you work hard toward achieving a result in the future as much as it requires you to be fully present, sincere, and committed *now*, with absolute honesty and a willingness to uncover and let go of *any* illusion that comes between you and the realization of Reality. Therefore, spirituality does not have to do with time or what can be achieved in time; it has to do *only and always* with the eternal present.

Aspiration is not so much a matter of the mind as of the heart, in that it is a reflection of what you cherish, love, and value most. You do not need to be reminded of what you truly love, only of what you do not love. And what you *actually* love is most truly reflected in your *actions,* not in what you feel, think, or say.

When aspiration lines up with unconditional follow-through and love, it becomes a very strong force in the universe. Only then are we unified and one-pointed enough for our aspiration to survive the winds of folly, fate, and circumstance.

## NEVER ABDICATE YOUR AUTHORITY

The third Foundation is *never abdicate your authority.* This means that *you take full responsibility for your life and never forfeit it over to someone else.* There is no such thing as riding the coattails of an enlightened being to enlightenment itself. A failure to understand this can lead (as so many have been led) to cultish fanaticism, fundamentalism, magical thinking, disappointment, disillusionment, and/or spiritual infancy.

While it is understandable that many people project their unresolved parental issues, relationship issues, authority issues, sexuality issues, as well as God issues onto their spiritual teacher (and are sometimes encouraged to do so by unscrupulous spiritual teachers), it is essential to understand that a spiritual teacher's role is to be a good and wise spiritual guide as well as an embodiment of the Truth that he or she points toward. While there may be deep respect, love, and even devotion to one's spiritual teacher, it is important not to abdicate all of your authority over to your spiritual teacher or project all divinity exclusively onto them. Your life belongs in your hands, not someone else's. Take responsibility for it.

There is a fine line between being truly open to the guidance of a spiritual teacher and regressing into a childish relationship where you abdicate your adulthood and project *all* wisdom and divinity onto the teacher. Each person needs to find a mature balance, being truly and deeply open to their spiritual guide without abdicating all of their authority.

The same can be applied to a spiritual teaching. A spiritual teaching is a finger pointing *toward* Reality; it is *not* Reality itself. To be in a true and mature relationship with a spiritual teaching requires you to *apply it,* not simply believe in it. Belief leads to various forms of fundamentalism and shuts down the curiosity and inquiry that are essential to open the way for awakening and what lies beyond awakening. A good spiritual teaching is something that you *work with* and *apply.* In doing so, it works on you (often in a hidden way) and helps reveal to you the Truth (and falseness) that lies within you.

What is it to not abdicate your own authority and yet not claim a false or self-centered authority that will lead you into delusion? I am afraid that I cannot tell you. You see, no one can tell you how not to deceive yourself. If in the deepest place within you, you want and desire Truth above all else, even though you go astray in a thousand different ways, you will find yourself somehow, again and again, being brought back to what is True.

And if you do not want and desire Truth above all else, well, you already know what that leads to.

## PRACTICE ABSOLUTE SINCERITY

To have genuine sincerity is absolutely necessary in the spiritual life. Sincerity encompasses the qualities of honesty, genuineness, and integrity. To be sincere does not mean to be perfect. In fact, the very effort to be perfect is itself insincere, because it is a way of avoiding seeing yourself as you are right now. To be able and willing to see yourself as you are, with all of your imperfections and illusions, requires genuine sincerity and courage. If we are constantly trying to hide from ourselves, we will never be able to awaken from our illusion of self.

In order to be sincere you must let go of being judgmental toward yourself. Being judgmental covers over your access to true sincerity and at times even masquerades *as* sincerity. True sincerity reveals a powerful form of clarity and discernment that is necessary in order to perceive yourself honestly without flinching or being held captive by your conditioned mind's judgments and defensiveness.

The capacity and willingness to be honest with yourself is your greatest guard against self-deception and deceit, and aligns you with your genuine aspiration. There is no greater challenge for a human being than to be completely honest with oneself as well as with others, and yet such honesty is absolutely necessary if we are ever to awaken from our dream of separation and live a truly genuine and undivided life.

## BE A GOOD STEWARD OF YOUR LIFE

Being a good steward of your life means that you are not using spirituality to avoid any aspect of yourself or your life. I have observed that it is very common for people involved in spirituality to unconsciously use it to avoid painful, troubling, dysfunctional, or fearful aspects of themselves or their lives. There is often a hope that if they just awaken to Reality, all of their challenges will disappear. While it is true that with the dawning of awakening many of what we regard as problems simply disappear, it would be wrong to assume that a taste of awakening automatically resolves every challenging aspect of human life.

Using spirituality to avoid challenging aspects of yourself or your day-to-day life can inhibit the dawning of spiritual enlightenment to a great extent, and will certainly inhibit its depth and stability. The Way of Liberation is a way of *completely* facing yourself and your life without withdrawing into denial, judgment, or magical thinking. It is a means of piercing through the veils of illusion and awakening to Truth.

To be a good steward of your life requires you to embrace every aspect of your life, inner and outer, pleasant and unpleasant. You do not necessarily need to face them all at once, just whatever arises in any given moment. Give each moment the attention, sincerity, and commitment that it deserves. A failure to do so is more costly than you can ever imagine.

Your life, *all* of your life, *is* your path to awakening. By resisting or not dealing with its challenges, you stay asleep to Reality. Pay attention to what life is trying to reveal to you. Say yes to its fierce, ruthless, and loving grace.

# CHAPTER TWO

# THREE ORIENTING IDEAS

*I*t is very easy to waste a lot of time and energy when one's spiritual pursuits are derailed into cul-de-sacs that have little or no relevance to spiritual awakening. The Three Orienting Ideas provide the conceptual framework on which the teaching rests and orient the mind toward the key principles that pertain to spiritual awakening. These Orienting Ideas give focus and direction to the Three Core Practices that are described later in this book.

## THE QUESTION OF BEING

Above the entrance to the Oracle of Delphi were written the words, "Know Thyself." Jesus came along and added a sense of urgency and consequence to the ancient idea when he said, "If you bring forth what is within you, what you bring forth will save you. If you do not bring forth what is within you, what you do not bring forth will destroy you."

What Jesus is saying is that spirituality is serious business, with serious consequences. Your life hangs precariously in the balance, teetering between a state of unconscious sleepwalking and eyes-wide-open spiritual enlightenment. The fact that most people do not see life this way testifies to how deeply asleep and in denial they truly are.

So what is it that we are to bring forth?

Within each of our forms lies the existential mystery of *being*. Apart from one's physical appearance, personality, gender, history, occupation, hopes and dreams, comings and goings, there lies an eerie silence, an abyss of stillness charged with an etheric presence. For all of our anxious business and obsession with triviality, we cannot completely deny this phantasmal essence at our core. And yet we do everything we can to avoid its stillness, its silence, its utter emptiness and radiant intimacy.

*Being* is that which disturbs our insistence on remaining in the life-numbing realm of our secret desperation. It is the itch that cannot be scratched, the whisper that will not be denied. To be, to truly *be,* is not a given.

Most of us live in a state where our *being* has long ago been exiled to the shadow realm of our silent anguish. At times *being* will break through the fabric of our unconsciousness to remind us that we are not living the life we could be living, the life that truly matters. At other times *being* will recede into the background silently waiting for our devoted attention. But make no mistake: *being*—your *being*—is the central issue of life.

To remain unconscious of *being* is to be trapped within an ego-driven wasteland of conflict, strife, and fear that only seems customary because we have been brainwashed into a state of suspended disbelief where a shocking amount of hate, dishonesty, ignorance, and greed are viewed as normal and sane. But they are not sane, not even close to being sane. In fact, nothing could be less sane and unreal than what we human beings call reality.

By clinging to what we know and believe, we are held captive by the movement of our conditioned thinking and imagination, all the while believing that we are perfectly rational and sane. We therefore continue to justify the reality of what causes us, as well as others, immeasureable amounts of pain and suffering.

Deep down we all suspect that something is very wrong with the way we perceive life but we try very, very hard not to notice it. And the way we remain blind to our frightful condition is through an obsessive and pathological denial of *being*—as if some dreadful fate would overcome us if we were to face the pure light of Truth and lay bare our fearful clinging to illusion.

It is within the dimension of *being* that Truth reveals itself— not the truth of mathematics or chemistry, philosophy or history, but a Truth that begins to disclose itself in those quiet moments when the ordinary routine of life suddenly becomes transparent to a sublime sense of meaning and significance unknown in common hours. Such vital and unexpected encounters with *being* indicate a Truth that lies just beneath the fabric of our ordinary lives, reminding us that the life we cling to may be more folly than we ever imagined, and that there is a Reality that has the power to unlock the mystery of our lives if we will just submit to its exacting command to leave behind our fearful commitment to security and life as we have known it.

We are all born with *being* veiled in obscurity. We may recognize the transparency of *being* shining in the eyes of an infant, but such *being* is not conscious of itself. It is veiled in an absence of self-awareness. Infants live in a magical world of unconscious *being,* while adults live in a world of egocentric separation and denial of *being.* Rectifying and restoring *being* to its true dominion and sovereignty is what spiritual awakening makes possible.

The question of *being* is everything. Nothing could be more important or consequential—nothing where the stakes run so high. To remain unconscious of *being* is to remain asleep to our own reality and therefore asleep to Reality at large. The choice is simple: awaken to *being* or sleep an endless sleep.

## THE FALSE SELF

The false self grows out of unconscious *being*. It is a fragmented amalgam of many selves tenuously bound together by a façade of normalcy. It is a divided house built upon an imaginary foundation, a broken-winged bird that cannot fly.

The false self is the greatest barrier (all barriers are imagined, of course) to the realization of our true identity of universal *being*. The false self is essentially a psychological *process* occurring in the mind that organizes, translates, and makes sense (or in many cases nonsense) of all incoming data from the senses. When this psychological process mixes together with the self-reflexive movement of consciousness, it produces a *sense* of self. This *sense* of self then pervades consciousness as a sort of perfume that causes the mind to mistake what is actually a psychological *process* for being an actual separate entity called *one's self*. This mistaken conclusion, that you are a distinct separate self, happens very early in life in a more or less automatic and unconscious way.

By identifying with a particular name that belongs to a particular body and mind, the self begins the process of creating a separate identity. Add in a complex jumble of ideas, beliefs, and opinions, along with some selective and often painful memories with which to create a past to identify with, as well as the raw emotional energy to hold it all together, and before you know it, you've got a very convincing—though divided—self.

This is not to say that in the development of a human being the false self has no purpose or use; it is simply to say that it has no existence whatsoever outside of the mind. The self develops in order that you may gain a healthy sense of individuation and autonomy that helps you navigate life in a way conducive to your survival and well-being. The problem is that few people ever develop true psychological autonomy, and even those who do are often so entranced by the false self that they never imagine its illusory nature or what lies beyond it. But once true autonomy is developed, the self is no longer needed, in the same way that infancy is no longer needed when you grow into adulthood. It may, however, be more accurate to say that it is the *autonomy* that is truly important, and that the false self is essentially an imaginary by-product of the self-reflexive mechanism of consciousness identifying itself with the endless movement of conditioned thinking.

The problem is that the self that you became convinced was the real you is a phantom that exists only as an abstraction in your mind—animated by the conflicted emotional energy of separation. It's about as real as last night's dream. And when you stop thinking it into existence, it has no existence at all. That's why it is false—which begs the question, who or what is the real you?

At the core of the false self is a void of deficiency derived from an essential turning away from one's own divinity, either out of natural development, despair, or simply by succumbing to the trance of the world with all its masks of deception and harsh obligation to conform to its insanity. The false self orbits around this vacuous abyss at its core, in silent terror of its nameless, faceless threat of oblivion.

The false self is both an obstacle and a doorway through which you must pass on your way to awakening to the dimension of *being*. As you pass *through* the void of self, the identification with self dies, either temporarily or permanently, and you are revealed (reborn) to be a *presence.* Presence is not a self in any conventional sense. It has no shape or form, no age or gender. It is an expression of universal *being,* the formless substance of existence. Presence is not subject to birth or death; it is not of the world of "things." It is the light and radiance of consciousness in which entire worlds arise and pass away.

Just as presence is an expression of *being,* so too is *being* an expression of the Infinite. The Infinite is ultimate Reality, and is beyond all conceptualizations and experiences. It is the ultimate ground of all *being,* all existence, all dimensions, and all perceptions. It is transcendent of all categories, all descriptions, all imaginings. It is beyond ego, self, presence, *being* (and *non-being*), and oneness, but it is not other than these either. Neither conceivable nor experience-able, the Infinite knows itself through a simple intuitive regard it has for itself in every aspect of itself. Thus the *only* thing that realizes the Infinite is the Infinite. And only such realization brings an end to the mind's restless search for God, Truth, and meaning.

## THE DREAM STATE

It is the nature of all dreams that the characters therein are so busy being . . . well, characters, that what lies *outside* the dream state eludes them. In fact, the very idea that there is an outside of their dream state, or that what they take to be real and meaningful *is* a dream state, is something that they would rarely even consider—at least, not until their dream becomes a very bad nightmare. And even then, very few will allow in the only thing that can save themselves from endless sleep.

So many are tied and bound to themselves that they cannot stop running from here to there and back again. Always on the lookout for something more, different, or better, they cannot see that they are getting nowhere at all. And they are getting absolutely nowhere faster and faster and with more and more ingenuity all the time.

Who are they? I am afraid that they are us.

The greatest dream that we can have is to forget that we are dreaming. Lost in our mind's imagined world of judgments, beliefs, and opinions, we are literally caught in a waking dream. For some it is a nightmare, for others a temporary reprieve in some imagined heaven. For most it is something in between.

But no matter what the current status of your dream may be, it will all come to an end someday when you least expect it. Suddenly the plot of your life will change or end altogether, and you will find yourself disoriented and wondering what happened and where it all went. Such abrupt changes in the direction and texture of our lives is one of the few certainties we have in life, and yet we keep believing that what we think about life has anything whatsoever to do with what life actually is.

We are so busy and obsessed with our restless thinking about everything and everyone that we have mistaken our thinking *about* everything and everyone *for* everything and everyone. This tendency to take our thoughts to be real is what keeps the dream state intact and keeps us trapped within its domain of unconsciousness and strife.

To many people the very idea that *what is* is more real than all of their beliefs and opinions *about what is* is hard to believe. But that's how it is when you are caught up in a dream. To you your dream is real because all of your thoughts confirm that it is real. But *what is* is more real than a thousand thoughts about how things should be. Life will conform neither to the story you tell yourself about it nor your interpretation of it. Believe a single thought that runs contrary to the way things are or have been and you suffer because of it. No exceptions!

15

This does not mean that you should not have any thoughts outside of *what is*. It only means that *what is* is the reality of *now*. If you think that people should be nice to one another, then by all means be nice. But when you project that belief onto the people and the world around you *as if it were an objective reality*, or worse still, as if it were their job to be nice to you, you put yourself at odds with *what is,* and suffering will surely follow.

Now imagine a world of billions of people. Each one of them has innumerable ideas, beliefs, and opinions that they believe to be true. And each one of those billions of people has *different* ideas, beliefs, and opinions that they absolutely believe in. They are all walking around seeing the same outside world, but inwardly they each live in a different world, in a different waking dream.

Is it any wonder we have trouble getting along?

To add complexity to this volatile mixture is the fact that there are also collective dream states where people of similar personal dreams gather together to form collective dream states. These are even harder spells to break out of, because collective dream states exist within a consensus (or agreed-upon) reality. In other words, it must be true because we all believe it to be true.

Thus is the state of humanity.

And the reality of universal *being,* your *being,* all *being,* remains exiled to the oblivion of unconsciousness.

# CHAPTER THREE

# THE CORE PRACTICES

*T*ruth is not *over there,* wherever *over there* is. Truth is neither housed in religious rituals nor secret doctrines, nor in a guru's touch or beatific smile, nor in exotic locations or ancient temples. Truth is quite literally the only thing that *does* exist. It is not hidden but in plain view, not lacking but abundantly present.

Absolute Truth is not a belief, not a religion, not a philosophy, not a momentary experience, and not a transient spiritual experience either. It is neither static nor in motion, neither good nor bad. It is other than all of that, more other than you can ever imagine. Truth cannot be touched by thought or imagined by the mind. It can only be found in the heart of universal *being. To know thy self is the key. To bring forth your being* is *The Way.*

In The Way of Liberation teachings there are three Core Practices that work in conjunction with the Five Foundations to assist in bringing forth and realizing timeless Truth. While these Core Practices may seem simple, do not be deceived—when combined and applied wholeheartedly they can be extremely powerful.

Our minds may believe that we need subtle and complex spiritual teachings to guide us to Reality, but we do not. In fact, the more complex the teaching is, the easier it is for the mind to hide from itself amidst the complexity while imagining that it is advancing toward enlightenment. But it is often only advancing in creating more and more intricate circles to walk around and around in.

The indispensable element of any spiritual teaching does not lie in the teaching but rather in the sincerity and fearlessness of the person who applies it. Even though at times you may feel quite lost in your own foolishness, as William Blake said, "A fool who persists in his folly will become wise."

Think of spiritual practice as a sort of "applied folly."

The Core Practices are something that you need to *get the feel of,* somewhat like getting the feel of balance when learning to ride a bicycle. They need to become a part of you to truly work. The attitude with which you apply them is as important as the practice itself—which is a way of saying that you need to find a way of applying the Core Practices that suits your temperament and personal style. No one can tell you exactly how to do this. You simply discover it by it trial and error. And the way that you utilize the Core Practices will evolve as your level of realization evolves.

You should not apply the Core Practices too willfully or with a great amount of struggle. They should be applied prayerfully; that is, with great sincerity and openness of mind and heart. While you may at times find yourself being very challenged by what these teachings reveal and at other times struggling with your own confusion and doubt, just remember that the element of grace is all-important and ever present. And it is often darkest just before the dawn.

All of our greatest breakthroughs seem to come by surprise, when we least expect them. Suddenly we are gifted, the clouds of confusion part, and we *see* with an uncommon clarity and freedom. Such grace is never held in abeyance, never earned or deserved. It is not given to some and not to others. Grace is ever present; it is only our openness to it that comes and goes. In one sense, *The Way of Liberation is a means of opening up to grace.*

The three Core Practices are meditation, inquiry, and contemplation.

## MEDITATION

In the various forms of esoteric spirituality, meditation is often either overemphasized or underemphasized. When meditation is overemphasized as the sole means to enlightenment, there is often too much focus placed on trying to attain a specific meditative *state*. Ultimate Reality is *not* a certain state of consciousness, no matter how wonderful or blissful. Reality is the ground of all *being*, unborn and undying eternity. It is as present in one experience or state of consciousness as in any other. Reality, or Truth, is that which is ultimately true in all states, at all times, in all locations.

On the other extreme are those teachings that underemphasize the value of meditation. The thinking is that since Reality is ever present in all situations at all times, there is nothing to attain by meditating. In fact, this thinking asserts, meditation will only emphasize the belief that one is separate from Reality and needs to do something to attain it. While there is logic in this viewpoint, it can lead to a type of fatalism and purely intellectual understanding that is counterproductive to true awakening. While there is no path or practice that leads directly to awakening, it is also true that what you *do* is vitally important in determining the course of your spiritual life. Balance is the key, effortless effort is the Way.

Meditation is neither a means to an end nor something to perfect. Meditation done correctly is an *expression* of Reality, not a path to it. Meditation done *incorrectly* is a perfect mirror of how you are resisting the present moment, judging it, or attaching to it. Meditation acts as a perfect mirror, which reflects your relationship with yourself, life, and the present moment. By becoming intimately aware of how you are resisting or attaching to the content of the present moment, and how futile it is to continue to do so, you may discover what it means to truly *drop all of your resistance to the present moment.*

In The Way of Liberation, meditation has a very specific definition, purpose, and application. Meditation is the art of *allowing everything to simply be* in the deepest possible way. In order to let everything be, we must *let go of the effort to control and manipulate our experience*—which means letting go of personal will. This cuts right to the heart of the egoic make-up, which seeks happiness through control, seeking, striving, and manipulation. Many forms of meditation are based on learning to control one's experience as a means of attaining peace. Such methods often lead to a dead end, where one only attains peace of mind as long as the ego is being constrained by meditative technique.

*The silence and stillness of meditation is the bedrock upon which this teaching rests.* It fosters an inward stability, objectivity, nonattachment, and depth of understanding unknown to the conceptual mind. Formal meditation is done best while sitting (or lying down if absolutely necessary) in a location where you will not be interrupted. The attitude conducive to meditation is one of surrender, effortlessness, and openness.

Meditation is more a form of silent prayer than a technique to master. When new to meditation, you may want to start with ten to fifteen minutes dedicated to being silent. When this amount of time feels comfortable, you may want to extend your meditation periods in five-minute increments until you can sit comfortably for thirty or forty minutes at a time. But even sitting in silence for fifteen to twenty minutes a day will begin to form an inner composure of stillness and stability within you.

It is important to understand that when doing meditation, you are *making a commitment to something other than your restless mind.* Meditation is not the time to be figuring things out or analyzing your experience. Neither should you be fighting your mind or trying to make it quiet. Just watch thoughts as you would watch clouds passing by in the sky. There is nothing personal about your thoughts. They are just phenomena passing through awareness. Meditation is not a technique to master; it is the highest form of prayer, a naked act of love and effortless surrender into the silent abyss beyond all knowing.

Meditation is not something restricted to times of formal seated meditation; it is most fundamentally an *attitude of being*—a resting in and as *being.* Once you get the *feel* of it, you will be able to tune into it more and more often during your daily life. Eventually, in the state of liberation, meditation will simply become your natural condition.

Below is a description of what I call True Meditation. Read it and let it reveal to you its true meaning by putting it into practice. Over time you will get a deeper and deeper understanding of what True Meditation is. You may want to read "True Meditation" each time just before you sit down to meditate until you feel that you have internalized the instructions.

## True Meditation

True Meditation has no direction or goal. It is pure wordless surrender, pure silent prayer. All methods aiming at achieving a certain state of mind are limited, impermanent, and conditioned. Fascination with states leads only to bondage and dependency. True Meditation is *effortless stillness, abidance as primordial being.*

True Meditation appears in consciousness spontaneously when awareness is not being manipulated or controlled. When you first start to meditate, you notice that attention is often being held captive by focusing on some object: on thoughts, bodily sensations, emotions, memories, sounds, etc. This is because the mind is conditioned to focus and contract upon objects. Then the mind compulsively interprets and tries to control what it is aware of (the object) in a mechanical and distorted way. It begins to draw conclusions and make assumptions according to past conditioning.

In True Meditation all objects (thoughts, feelings, emotions, memories, etc.) are left to their natural functioning. This means that no effort should be made to focus on, manipulate, control, or suppress any object of awareness. In True Meditation the emphasis is on being awareness—not on being aware of objects, but on resting as *conscious being* itself. In meditation you are not trying to change your experience; you are changing your *relationship to* your experience.

As you gently relax into awareness, the mind's compulsive contraction around objects will fade. Silence of *being* will come more clearly into consciousness as a welcoming to rest and abide. An attitude of open receptivity, free of any goal or anticipation, will facilitate the presence of silence and stillness to be revealed as your natural condition.

As you effortlessly rest into stillness more profoundly, awareness becomes free of the mind's compulsive habit of control, contraction, and identification. Awareness returns to its natural condition of *conscious being*, absolute unmanifest potential—the silent abyss beyond all knowing.

## Some Common Questions about Meditation

**Q.** It seems that the central instruction in True Meditation is simply to abide as silent, still awareness. However, I often find that I am caught in my mind. Is it OK to use a more directed meditation like following my breath so that I have something to focus on which will help me to not get lost in my mind?

**A.** It is perfectly OK to use a more directed technique such as following your breath, or using a simple mantra or centering prayer, if you find that it helps you to not get lost in thought. But always be inclined toward less and less technique. Make time during each meditation period to simply rest *as silent, still* awareness. True Meditation is progressively letting go of the meditator without getting lost in the mind.

~

**Q.** What should I do if an old painful memory arises during meditation?

**A.** Old memories, hurts, fears, angers, resentments, etc., can arise in meditation. Simply allow them to arise without resisting, analyzing, judging, or denying them. Just watch them without getting involved. See that they do not define who you are. They are pockets of unconsciousness arising to be purified in the light of awareness and released from your system. Allow the light of *being* to set suffering free.

~

**Q.** When I meditate I sometimes experience a lot of fear. Sometimes it overwhelms me and I don't know what to do.

**A.** It is useful when experiencing fear in meditation to anchor your attention in something very grounding such as your breath or even the bottoms of your feet. But don't fight against the fear, because this will only increase it. Imagine that you are the Buddha under the Bodhi tree, or Christ in the desert, remaining perfectly still and unmoved by the body-mind's nightmare. It may feel very real, but it is really nothing more than a convincing illusion. In absolute effortless stillness, fear will pass away of its own accord.

~

**Q.** What should I do when I get an insight or sudden understanding of a situation during meditation?
**A.** Simply receive what is given with gratitude, without holding onto anything. Trust that it will still be there when you need it.

~

**Q.** I find that my mind is spontaneously forming images, almost like a waking dream. Some of them I like, while others are just random and annoying. What should I do?
**A.** Focus attention on your breathing down in your belly. This will help you to not get lost in the images of the mind. Hold the simple intention to rest in the imageless, silent source prior to all images, thoughts, and ideas.

~

**Q.** I am experiencing a lot of energy surging through my body when I meditate, and even when I am not meditating. Sometimes it is very pleasant but at other times it makes me feel agitated and keeps me awake at night. What is it?
**A.** It is not uncommon that at some point in your spiritual life you will experience various forms of intense energy. Do not become fascinated by the energy and do not try to suppress or control it, because doing so will only tend to intensify it. Root

your attention in that state which is prior to all forms of energy. Rest in silence, stillness, and emptiness, prior to the energies of body and mind. Root your attention in the lower abdomen. This will help ground and integrate the energy.

It may also be useful to do some very grounding activities. Take quiet walks in nature, exercise, massage the bottoms of your feet, etc. Anything that feels grounding and energetically calming will help. It will take some time for your body and nervous system to adapt to a greater volume of energy flowing through you. Be patient. It often takes months or years for the nervous system to adapt to the new influx of energy.

~

**Q.** Sometimes I feel a depth of silence where all intention falls away and even the instruction to allow everything to be or to rest as awareness feels unnecessary. Is it OK to let all intention and technique fall away?

**A.** At times, even the most subtle intention or technique will naturally drop away on its own when your meditation reaches a certain depth of stillness and simplicity. When you can let go of all intention and technique and not get lost in the mind or fall into a foggy or dull state of awareness, True Meditation is spontaneously happening. The ultimate form of meditation is when the meditator falls completely away.

## INQUIRY

The sacred dimension is not something that you can know through words and ideas any more than you can learn what an apple pie tastes like by eating the recipe. The modern age has forgotten that facts and information, for all their usefulness, are not the same as truth or wisdom, and certainly not the same as direct experience. We have lost touch with the intuitive wisdom born of silence and stillness. To hold a question inwardly in silent and patient waiting is an art rarely mastered these days. Inquiry is a bridge between the ego and the soul, and beyond to the Infinite. (I am using the term *soul* here to mean *the essence, presence, or beingness that you are.*)

Inquiry is not in any sense anti-intellectual or anti-rational; it is trans-rational. That is, it has the power to take you beyond both the conceptual mind as well as conditioned egocentric thinking. Although rooted in stillness, inquiry is the dynamic counterpoint to True Meditation. Meditation is soft, allowing surrender, while inquiry demands bold and fearless questioning.

Inquiry is a way of addressing the deepest existential issues confronting every human being: Who or what am I? What is life? What happens after death? What is God? What is the absolute Truth of existence? Or simply, Do I know with *absolute certainty* that this current thought, belief, opinion, interpretation, or judgment is true?

The common element to inquiry is Truth. What is Truth?

The Truth question does not arise from, or pertain to, the various agendas of the ego. It is of the utmost importance that inquiry not become subject to the ego's various drives and motivations. The underlying drives of the ego are to feel better and to survive. But inquiry belongs entirely to the realm of the soul, that dimension of *being* born of stillness and light that seeks Truth *for its own sake.*

The first focus of inquiry centers on *being. Being* is the key that unlocks the kingdom. Who or what am I? Apart from body, mind, belief, occupation, gender, role, memory, or history, what am I? Exactly what is "I"?

Remove all that the I is not. Strip the I of *all* the masks it wears. What's left? Something? Nothing? What's aware of that?

In your *direct experience,* is some-*thing* aware, or is no-*thing* aware? Is someone aware or is no one aware?

Trace the thread of inquiry *silently and patiently* back through all of your identifications, all of your beliefs about yourself, all of your hidden judgments and assumptions about who and what you are. Take your time. Look deeply into each of these questions. Let the questions remove all that you are not. Let them undo all that you ever imagined yourself to be, all that you thought you should be, all that anyone ever told you to be. Trace the thread of inquiry back through all of your imagined identities. Follow the thread back through all that is imagined, clung to, or run from. Then *be still.* Rest in the contemplative silence and let the unknown workings of grace run their course.

The realization of Truth and Reality can never be created by the mind; it always comes as a gift of grace. Inquiry clears away misperceptions and illusions, making one available to the movements of grace.

The question of *being* opens the doorway to Reality and Truth, but is by no means the only question for inquiry. Question everything! Leave no stone unturned, no assumption unexamined, no form of denial left intact.

Investigate each question slowly and deliberately. Place each question into the stillness of your being. Do not grasp for quick answers. Don't jump to conclusions. Instead, let each question reveal your hidden beliefs and opinions. Let it reveal whatever you are holding on to and believing that is at odds with *what is.* Look for all the ways that attaching to your mind causes you and others to suffer. Bring each question the mind poses into the ground of stillness. Meditate on it, ponder it; take your time. Don't answer it with your mind. Be still with only the question. Be very, very still.

Filled with the love of Truth, don't be surprised if inquiry begins to consume all of your hidden assumptions, all of your beliefs, all of your opinions, all of your judgments, all that you have learned secondhand from others. And don't be surprised if most of your spiritual ideas are consumed as well, for it is our spiritual ideas that most effectively protect us from the truly spiritual experience.

Your greatest aid is your sincerity and desire for Truth above all else. You may be shocked over and over again by the depth of illusion that you find and uncover within yourself, but never fixate on it or judge yourself. Accept, forgive, and move on, for your true *being* is infinite and absolute. It exists as much now as it ever did or ever will. Stand still in the sacred conflagration of inquiry and let it open you to the seat of all wisdom born of spirit. Only Truth will survive; all else will perish.

It is a sad thing that so few give the full measure of their lives to Truth. Most only go so far, and then settle for less than a total surrender of all separation. In the end we all get what we value most, and if we don't like what we have gotten, we had better take an honest look at what we are valuing.

But never for a moment is Truth lacking. Never is there more or less Truth present, or more or less availability. Truth is in abundant supply at all times, in all situations. It is simply awaiting recognition. And it has all of time on its side.

Question your thoughts. Question your stories. Question your assumptions. Question your opinions. Question your conclusions. Question them all into utter emptiness, stillness, and joy. The keys to freedom are in *your* hands. Use them.

## Some Common Questions about Inquiry

**Q**. Inquiry often feels very intellectual to me and I just tend to get lost in my mind. Is there a way to inquire without it becoming so lost in the mind?

**A.** Yes. There two aspects of inquiry, and it's very important to understand both of them. The first aspect of inquiry is what I call "taking the backward step." The purpose of the first aspect of inquiry is to remove or *step back* from prior conditioned thinking. You are not looking for answers as much as you are revealing and removing prior conditioned thoughts, ideas, and beliefs *to make way for* a deeper realization. For example, through such observation you can come to see that you are not the thoughts in your mind. By removing the false belief that any thought can tell you what you are, you make space for a deeper understanding to reveal itself.

Having revealed and cleared out the false ideas of mind, you are now ready to rest in the stillness of *being*.

In the second aspect of inquiry, you are endeavoring to access the intuitive clarity and wisdom that is housed in stillness at the root of consciousness. I call it the *realm of grace* because the wisdom that flows out of it is always received as a gift, as an "aha" of pure understanding. Having revealed and cleared out the false ideas of mind, you are now ready *to rest in the stillness of being,* without imposing thought or seeking in thought.

∿

**Q.** Sometimes inquiry feels very alive and vital to me, but at other times it feels more mechanical because my heart isn't into it. Is inquiry something I need to be engaged in all the time?

**A.** In order for inquiry to be authentic, you need to feel like it is of vital interest to you. So no, you do not need to be inquiring all the time. It is a tool that is there whenever a vital question arises for you. But inquiry is also much more than a technique; it is an *attitude.*

Inquiry is an attitude of curiosity that lives within you, and it is a reflection of your desire to know Truth and the nature of Reality. Inquiry also takes a type of courage that is willing to ask big questions that may shake up the very foundations of your life and put you face-to-face with issues you might rather avoid.

So while you won't always be using the technique of inquiry, it is vitally important to live with the attitude of curiosity and courage that is at the heart of inquiry.

⌒

*Inquiry is the art of questioning all of one's assumptions, beliefs, and interpretations* as a means of opening up space in the mind for intuitive wisdom to arise. Once space is opened up, simply rest the question in the stillness of conscious *being.*

Watch. Keep faithful vigil with the unknown. The vital moments of breakthrough come when you least expect them.

## CONTEMPLATION

We have long ago forgotten what it means to contemplate something. With the click of a computer mouse we can get the answer, or what promises to be the answer, to almost any question we can imagine. All of the world's most ancient spiritual teachings are but a click or download away, and yet we remain so lost to ourselves, so cut off from what nourishes the soul, that we are collectively suffocating under the weight of our ignorance and alienation from the sacred dimension of Life.

The modern age has forgotten that facts and information, for all their usefulness, are not the same as wisdom—and certainly not the same as the direct experience of Reality. We have lost touch with the intuitive wisdom born of silence and stillness, and we are left stranded in a sea of information that cannot deliver on its promise of ever-increasing happiness and fulfillment.

Contemplation is the art of holding a word or a phrase patiently in the silence and stillness of awareness until it begins to disclose deeper and deeper meanings and understandings. Contemplation has the power to transcend beyond (not regress back from) the limits of analytical thought and logic, and open consciousness up to an order of wisdom and Truth that can only be described as revelation.

I have included some useful short phrases in this section, but any part of this book can be used as an object for contemplation. Take *a short phrase* as your object of contemplation and simply hold it in your awareness for some time. Do not analyze or philosophize about it. And do not get lost in your imagination either. Just hold the phrase in awareness. Then be still. Let its meaning germinate within you. Then bring the word or phrase back into awareness again. Hold it there for some time, and then let it go and be still again. With a little practice you will get the hang of it and find your own rhythm.

While contemplation may seem quite simple, it can be very powerful. In the Zen tradition, phrases, questions, or short teaching stories called *koans* are used as objects of contemplation and meditation to great and powerful effect in sparking awakening, revelation, and enlightenment. In fact, most esoteric systems of spirituality have used various forms of contemplation to elicit moments of revelation.

Below are some phrases to use as objects of contemplation. They begin with phrases designed to spark certain psychological insights and progress to phrases designed to bring about deeper and deeper realizations and revelations of a more fundamental or spiritual nature. The final series of phrases pertains to the absolute nature of Reality, the Infinite.

## Thought and Freedom from Suffering

⌒

There is no such thing as
an absolutely True thought.

*This doesn't mean that some thoughts are not truer than others, only that no thought is absolutely True.*

⌒

*What is* is what's happening
*before* you have a thought about it.

*Notice the difference between what your mind thinks about this moment, and this moment as it is before you have any thought about it.*

⌒

Suffering occurs when you
believe in a thought that is at odds with
what is, what was, or what may be.

*Experience this moment free of your mind's interpretations of it.*

⌒

*You* are not your story.
*They* are not your story about them.
*The world* is not your story about the world.

~

Suffering is how Life tells you
that you are resisting or misperceiving
what is real and true.

*It is the way Life suggests that you are not in harmony with what is.*

~

Deeper understanding and insight flow forth from a quiet mind.

~

To be happy is to
live as the unknown.

~

All true knowing arises out of the unknown
and is an expression of the unknown.

## The Nature of *Being*

~

To look within and not find yourself as a self
is the beginning of finding yourself as a presence *(being)*.

~

*Being* (or spirit) is universal
and exists prior to all conditions,
all points of view, all objects of consciousness,
and all subjects as well.

~

*Being* is the true nature
of everything.

⁓

Being the nature of everything,
there is nothing outside of *being*.

⁓

*Being* is self-cognizant and aware. Right now!

⁓

*Being* doesn't explain everything;
*being* is the true nature of everything.

⁓

The only thing that realizes *being* is *being* itself.

⁓

There is only *being* living itself
through you, as you, and as all that exists.

⁓

*Being* is unborn and uncreated—
the source and substance of all.

⁓

*Being* is our original condition,
prior to all egoic antics, prior to all thought,
prior to all description,
prior to past, present, and future.

⁓

That *beingness* which is
prior to the world of space and time
is here, now, and always.
It is a single drop of rain, a leaf falling from a tree,
a single heartbeat.
It is the world-less world,
the substance of emptiness.

~

I AM is pure *being*.
It is the ultimate confession of Reality
echoing throughout eternity.

## The Infinite

~

Beyond ego is universal *being;* beyond *being* is the Infinite.

~

The Infinite is pure formless potential,
prior to *being* and *non-being,* life and death,
form and formlessness.

~

The Infinite is neither one nor many,
neither dualistic nor nondualistic,
neither worldly nor spiritual,
neither self nor other.

~

The Infinite knows itself
through a simple intuitive regard it has for itself
in every aspect of itself.
Thus it knows itself as utterly unknowable
and absolutely present.

~

To realize the Infinite is to lose your inner world.

~

To lose your inner world is eternal silence.
It is to become the shining.

~

All is well,
and more well than can be imagined.

# CONCLUSION

*T*he enlightenment I speak of is not simply a realization, not simply the discovery of one's true nature. This is just the beginning—the point of entry into an inner revolution. Realization does not guarantee this revolution; it simply makes it possible.

## AN INNER REVOLUTION

What is this inner revolution? To begin with, revolution is not static; it is alive, ongoing, and continuous. It cannot be grasped or made to fit into any conceptual model. Nor is there any path to this inner revolution, for it is neither predictable nor controllable and has a life all its own. This revolution is a breaking away from the old, repetitive, dead structures of thought and perception that humanity finds itself trapped in. Realization of the ultimate Reality is a direct and sudden existential awakening to one's true nature that opens the door to the possibility of an inner revolution. Such a revolution requires an ongoing emptying out of the old structures of consciousness and the birth of a living and fluid intelligence. This intelligence restructures your entire being, body, mind, and perception. This intelligence cuts

37

the mind free of its old structures that are rooted within the totality of human consciousness. If one cannot become free of the old conditioned structures of human consciousness, then one is still in a prison.

Having an awakening to one's true nature does not necessarily mean that there will be an ongoing revolution in the way one perceives, acts, and responds to life. The moment of awakening shows us what is ultimately True and real as well as revealing a deeper possibility in the way that life can be lived from an undivided and unconditioned state of *being*. But the moment of awakening does not guarantee this deeper possibility, as many who have experienced spiritual awakening can attest to. Awakening opens a door inside to a deep inner revolution, but in no way guarantees that it will take place. Whether it takes place or not depends on many factors, but none more important and vital than an earnest and unambiguous intention for Truth above and beyond all else. This earnest intention toward Truth is what all spiritual growth ultimately depends upon, especially when it transcends all personal preferences, agendas, and goals.

This inner revolution is the awakening of an intelligence not born of the mind but of an inner silence of mind, which alone has the ability to uproot all of the old structures of one's consciousness. Unless these structures are uprooted, there will be no creative thought, action, or response. Unless there is an inner revolution, nothing new and fresh can flower. Only the old, the repetitious, the conditioned, will flower in the absence of this revolution. But our potential lies beyond the known, beyond the structures of the past, beyond anything that humanity has established. Our potential is something that can flower only when we are no longer caught within the influence and limitations of the known. Beyond the realm of the mind, beyond the limitations of humanity's conditioned consciousness, lies that which can be called the sacred. And it is from the sacred that a new and fluid consciousness is born that wipes away the old and brings to life the flowering of a living and undivided expression of *being*. Such an expression is neither personal nor impersonal, neither spiritual nor worldly, but rather the flow and flowering of existence beyond all notions of self.

So let us understand that Reality transcends all of our notions about Reality. Reality is neither Christian, Hindu, Jewish, Advaita Vedanta, nor Buddhist. It is neither dualistic nor nondualistic, neither spiritual nor nonspiritual. We should come to know that there is more Reality and sacredness in a blade of grass than in all of our thoughts and ideas about Reality. When we perceive from an undivided consciousness, we will find the sacred in every expression of life. We will find it in our teacup, in the fall breeze, in the brushing of our teeth, in each and every moment of living and dying. Therefore we must leave the entire collection of conditioned thought behind and let ourselves be led by the inner thread of silence and intuitive awareness, beyond where all paths end, to that place of sacredness where we go innocently or not at all, not once but continually.

One must be willing to stand alone—in the unknown, with no reference to the known or the past or any of one's conditioning. One must stand where no one has stood before in complete nakedness, innocence, and humility. One must stand in that dark light, in that groundless embrace, unwavering and true to the Reality beyond all self, not just for a moment but forever without end; for then that which is sacred, undivided, and whole is born within consciousness and begins to express itself. That expression is the salvation of the whole. It is the *activity* of an inward revolution brought down into time and space.

# EPILOGUE

*I*magine that one morning you wake up, and as you open your eyes, you suddenly realize that everything is not as it used to be. And I mean everything! Not that anything looks different to the eye, but rather that what is doing the looking has somehow changed or mutated in some strange and unpredictable way. And there you are, just stepping out of bed, wondering if you are actually still fast asleep under the covers dreaming this strange dream.

But you are not dreaming, and you know it. You know that you are not dreaming with a certainty unlike you have ever felt before. In fact, you realize that every moment of every day of your life up to just a few moments ago was spent in a state of unconscious sleepwalking that felt so real and so true that you had never even thought to question its validity. The consensus opinion is that once you are out of bed and walking around, you are very awake. But it simply isn't true.

How did you not notice something so obvious?

But that's not all, not by a long shot. Imagine that as you are noticing this strange change taking place within yourself, that something even more unsettling occurs to you: that there is no *inside* of you; in fact, there is no self to be inside of. So you start looking for yourself. How on earth did you lose yourself? After all, you're not like a pair of slippers that you can just misplace. You are you, and you must be around here somewhere. Mustn't you?

But no matter where you look inside, you cannot find yourself as anyone, or anywhere in particular. All the old thoughts and all the old memories no longer pertain to you yourself. They are empty—empty of self, that is. Even that face in the mirror that seems so familiar is without a self. It never had one, except the one you made up in your mind. And even the one you made up never really had a self to begin with.

You look out the window and . . . there is no *out there*. Everywhere you look is somehow in here, wherever here is. So you look through the window and everything out there, or over there, is inside of you—and not just inside of you, but *is you*. The ground and trees and fence over there, as well as the sky overhead and the white puffy clouds, everything is you. It doesn't make sense but it's about as obvious as breathing. What's a self that's the same as everything else?

This is strange indeed.

Imagine that you're now walking down the sidewalk listening to the neighbors talking to each other, when it occurs to you that they are making it all up. All the stories, all the little judgments, all the firmly held opinions, all the "he should haves," and "she should haves," and "what I think is . . ." are all made up, but taken to be real. It's like they're playing make-believe but forgetting that it's all imagination, or getting lost in last night's dream.

How could they be taking what they're saying so seriously, as if any of it mattered or had any basis in Reality? How could they not see? But they don't see. To them it's their reality, the only one that they know, or probably ever will know. How very strange.

Now imagine that you stop to sit on a bench in the park. As you sit there everything stops, absolutely stops. Your mind is so still and quiet that you can hear dust particles floating in the air. Suddenly you are falling, and falling, and falling. There is no ground below or sky overhead, just a crushing thunderous silence, racing faster and faster. You suddenly realize that it's going to kill you, rip you limb from limb and explode your lungs into dust. There's no way out, no possible means of survival. And so you do the only thing there is to do.

Surrender.

All goes blank and empty, more empty than limitless space.

Prior to life and death, you blink out of (or is it into?) existence. Timelessness is all there is, all there ever was, or could be. Eternity reigns supreme, and is radiantly present in every particle of *being*.

Something unborn and undying stirs to life and opens its eyes—your eyes. You or It is still sitting on the park bench. It is smiling, radiant, and content. A little girl on roller skates passes by. The sun glitters through the aspen leaves as an old man smokes his pipe on a footbridge crossing over a stream that feeds into a pond filled with goldfish.

Everywhere you look is emptiness. Each "thing" is a veil, a shroud, cloaking Infinity. Nothing is as it seems, and everything is exactly as it is. Somehow perfect in all its apparent chaos, Infinity prevails. You know with exact precision that there is nothing else—nothing could be other than this vast and absolute void, this pure and Infinite Potential, this unborn and unformed Infinity.

You reflect back over your life and realize that everything that ever happened or ever could happen, from birth to all of the ups and downs of this ephemeral life, to the strange realizations of spiritual awakening, to this exact moment outside of time, was and is the momentary display—a blip, really—of Infinity's limitless potential coming into, and going out of, existence.

An old friend finds you sitting on the bench in the park. She sits down beside you and asks, "What are you up to?" You love her as friends do, but what can you say? You're already speechless, and as quiet inside as the dead. She doesn't know it, but you're in two different worlds, strangely intersecting here on this park bench. How do you reach across infinity to communicate with her?

For a moment you strain inside for the words with which to respond. There is a silent pause—is she onto you? Does she suspect something is different? A cool breeze caresses your face and the universe smiles inside you. "Oh, nothing really," you say. "Absolutely Nothing."

# SUMMARY OF THE TEACHING

Be still.
Question every thought.
Contemplate the source of Reality.

*A*nd keep your eyes open. You never know when something that seems entirely insignificant will split your whole world wide open into eternal delight.

# THE WAY OF LIBERATION
## STUDY GROUPS

*I* encourage those interested in practicing The Way of Liberation to form or find a study group that meets regularly to explore, study, discuss, and put these teachings into practice. While studying the teachings alone will feel right for some people, studying the teachings and sharing your experience with others in a group can be very useful. Exploring these teachings with others can open you to new and added perspectives, as well as providing compassionate support for each other.

A Way of Liberation study group should be a safe and loving environment to gather in mutual exploration of the teachings.

It is of the utmost importance to remember that The Way is not itself the Truth but a means of realizing Truth. The Truth lies within you, not anywhere else. By studying and putting The Way into practice, you are studying, bringing forth, and realizing the Truth within you.

### SUGGESTIONS FOR THE FORMAT

Anyone can form a study group and come up with their own format. The Way of Liberation study groups form and run independently of either Adyashanti or Open Gate Sangha. I do, however, suggest that each meeting be centered on a particular aspect of The Way of Liberation teaching that was chosen during the previous group meeting. I also suggest that each meeting include some time for silent meditation (preferably at the beginning) as well as discussion about the particular teaching that was chosen for that meeting.

## GUIDELINES

The following are guidelines for The Way of Liberation study groups to embody. They are meant to reflect an attitude of mutual openness, compassion, and support.

1. Study groups should be safe and compassionate environments in which to explore, share, and put into practice the Way of Liberation teachings.

2. All study groups should be free of charge, unless the group is renting a space to meet in.

3. No one should act as a *teacher* or try to dominate a group.

4. When someone is sharing their experience, do not judge what they are sharing. *If asked for,* give feedback by speaking only from your own experience. Do not try to be the teacher.

5. Everyone who comes to a meeting for the first time should be given a copy of these guidelines. If a study group does not follow these guidelines, I suggest you either stop attending it or form your own study group.

For a listing of The Way of Liberation study groups (or to add your group to the list) visit *www.adyashanti.org/wayofliberation.*

# RECOMMENDED READINGS

Adyashanti recommends the following for further reading and exploration of the themes in this book:

## Grace and Suffering

*Falling into Grace* by Adyashanti
Published by Sounds True
© 2011 Adyashanti

## Meditation and Inquiry

*True Meditation* by Adyashanti
Published by Sounds True
© 2006 Adyashanti

## Life after Awakening

*The End of Your World* by Adyashanti
Published by Sounds True
© 2008 Sounds True

These books, and many free articles and downloads, are available at *www.adyashanti.org.*

# ACKNOWLEDGMENTS

*A* big thank-you to Jerilyn Munyon—your tireless encouragement, support, and clear feedback are a gift beyond measure. A big thanks to Maja Apolonia Rodé—your creative and loving gifts touch every aspect of this book from editing, to layout and design, and beyond. Your enthusiastic support of this project was a true blessing. A deep bow of gratitude to Julie Donovan, for all of your dedication to the editing and fine details of bringing this book to life. I also give a deep bow of gratitude to Susan Kurtz, for your wonderful work on the design of this book and for all of your quiet and creative talents. From the bottom of my heart, thank you all.

# ABOUT THE AUTHOR

*A*dyashanti, author of *Falling into Grace, True Meditation, The End of Your World, Emptiness Dancing,* and *My Secret Is Silence,* is an American-born spiritual teacher devoted to serving the awakening of all beings. His teachings are an open invitation to stop, inquire, and recognize what is true and liberating at the core of all existence. Asked to teach in 1996 by his Zen teacher of 14 years, Adyashanti offers teachings that are free of any tradition or ideology. "The Truth I point to is not confined within any religious point of view, belief system, or doctrine, but is open to all and found within all."

Based in California, where he lives with his wife, Mukti, Adyashanti teaches throughout North America, Europe, and Australia. For more information, please visit *www.adyashanti.org.*

The Reality that
these teachings are
pointing toward is not
hidden or secret or
far away. . . .
At this very moment,
Reality and completeness
are in plain sight.

*~ Adyashanti*